METROPOLITAN BOROUGH OF WIRRAL

Please return this book to the Library from which it was borrowed before the last date stamped. If not in demand books may be renewed by letter, telephone or in person. Fines will be charged on overdue books at the rate currently determined by the Borough Council.

WILFRED OWEN LIBRARY

Acc 2 08

665

PECHEY, R.

Focus on Gas

S382438

665

PECHEY, R.

Focus on Gas

S382438

METROPOLITAN BOROUGH OF WIRRAL SCHOOL LIBRARY SERVICE

DEPARTMENT OF LEISURE SERVICES LIBRARIES AND ARTS

Gas

The three main fuels used today are oil, gas and coal. This book focuses on gas and examines the role it plays as an energy source; in the home, in industry and even in transport. Where is natural gas found and how are the many other gases made? We explore the origins of gas, from deep in the earth's crust, together with its safe distribution through a vast network of pipelines. Although we think of gas predominantly as a fuel, it has other functions. It is extremely important in the chemical industry as a raw material, helping to produce plastics and fertilizers. As the gas reserves of the world decline, we also look to the future and consider alternative gases, such as biogas and substitute natural gas.

Roger Pechey is a journalist who has worked on energy-related publications for many years. He is currently editor of *Gas World*.

Focus on
GAS

Roger Pechey

Focus on Resources series

Alternative Energy
Coal
Coffee
Cotton
Dairy Produce
Fruit
Gas
Gold and Silver
Grain
Iron and Steel
Meat
Nuclear Fuel

Oil
Paper
Plastics
Rice
Rubber
Seafood
Soya
Sugar
Tea
Timber
Water
Wool

Frontispiece *A night view of a North Sea gas terminal in Yorkshire, England.*

First published in 1986 by
Wayland (Publishers) Ltd
61 Western Road, Hove
East Sussex BN3 1JD, England

© Copyright 1986 Wayland (Publishers) Ltd

Phototypeset by Kalligraphics Ltd, Redhill, Surrey
Printed in Italy by G. Canale & C.S.p.A., Turin
Bound in Great Britain at The Bath Press, Avon

British Library Cataloguing in Publication Data

Pechey, Roger
  Focus on gas. – (Focus on resources series)
  1. Gas, Natural – Juvenile literature
  I. Title
  333.8′233   HD9581.A2

ISBN 0–85078–657–6

Contents

1. What are the fuel gases? 6
2. Exploration for gas 8
3. Discovery and appraisal 10
4. Transmission 12
5. Distribution 14
6. The history of town gas 16
7. Gas in the home 18
8. Gas in industry and commerce 20
9. Metering 22
10. Safety and gas detection 24
11. How gas is stored 26
12. Liquefied natural gas (LNG) 28
13. Liquefied petroleum gas (LPG) 30
14. Compressed natural gas (CNG) 32
15. Substitute natural gas (SNG) 34
16. Biogas 36
17. The manufacture of chemicals 38
18. International trade 40
19. Gas industries around the world 42

Facts and figures 44
Glossary 46
Sources of further information 47
Books to read 47
Index 48

1. What are the fuel gases?

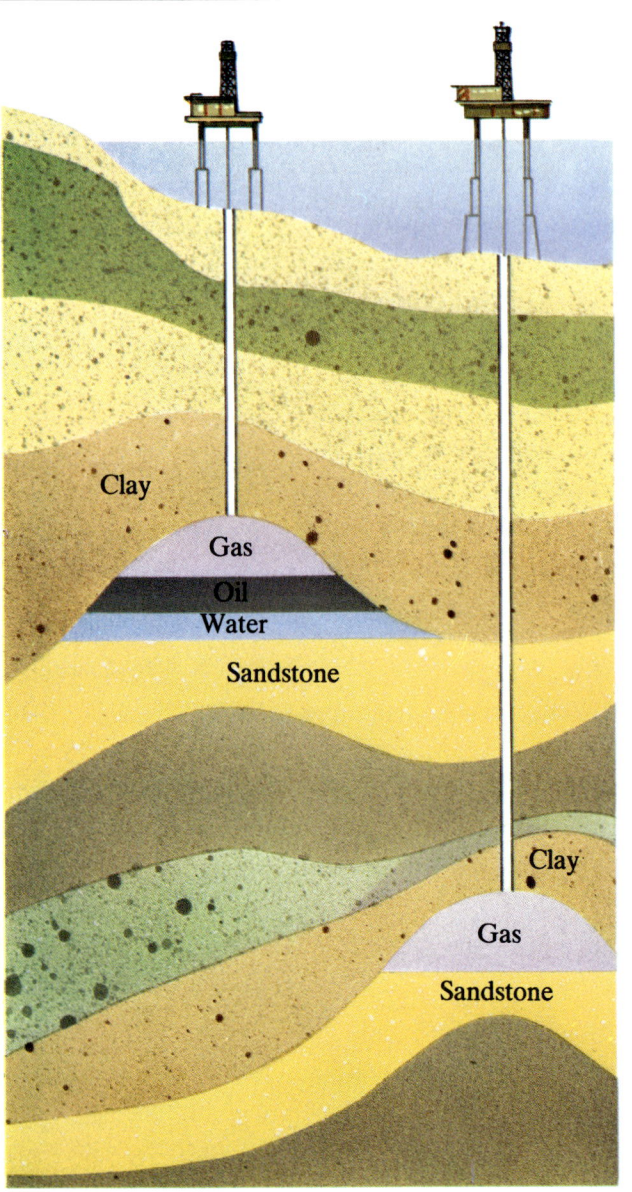

The fuel gases are known as hydrocarbon gases as they all contain hydrogen and carbon. These two elements also form the major part of all living things.

This is no coincidence. The fuel gases were formed many millions of years ago from the decay of plants and sea creatures. When they died they settled on the sea-bed and were later covered by layers of sediment and silt.

The weight of rocks pressing down on this debris caused high temperatures and pressures to build up. The effect of this was very similar to a pressure cooker, cooking the plants and sea creatures into mixtures of crude oils and hydrocarbon gases.

Today we find crude oils and gases by drilling exploration wells deep into the earth's surface. In a chemical sense, the gases and crude oils are members of the same family. The differences depend on the numbers of atoms of hydrogen and carbon in each molecule.

The simplest molecule of a fuel gas is methane, which has one carbon atom surrounded by four hydrogen atoms. Natural gas largely consists of methane.

This cross-section through the earth's crust shows in which type of rock formations gas may be found.

Next is ethane with two carbon atoms surrounded by six hydrogen atoms. As we add more carbon and hydrogen atoms, we move on to propane and butane.

Molecules containing five, six and seven carbon atoms are no longer gases. They are liquids and are the first members of the crude oil family which can contain as many as 20 or more carbon atoms in each molecule.

Hydrocarbon gases contain hydrogen and carbon atoms in differing numbers. Molecules with four or more carbon atoms are the first of the crude oils.

Above *This man is drilling for oil; gas and oil are often found in the same reservoirs.*

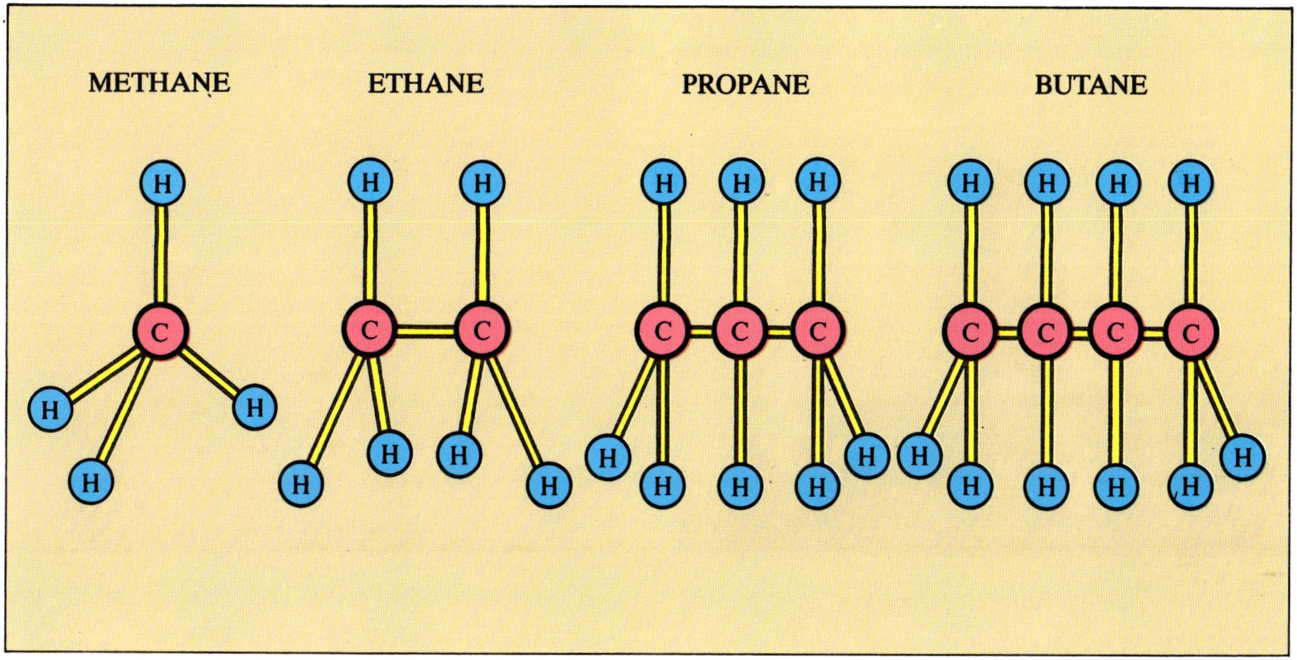

METHANE ETHANE PROPANE BUTANE

2. Exploration for gas

Oil and gas are often found in the same reservoir since they were formed by the same process. Natural gas is usually found as a 'gas cap' above the oil reservoir. When oil companies start to explore for oil and gas, they look for layers of soft permeable rock covered with a much harder impermeable layer.

The permeable rock has many tiny holes, like a sponge, which can absorb the oil and gas. The hard impermeable rock, known as the cap rock, acts like a lid which traps the oil and gas.

Before drilling for oil, it is essential to carry out a survey of the rock layers to decide which areas look promising. One of the most common ways of doing this is through seismic surveys.

A seismic survey unit testing for gas in the countryside.

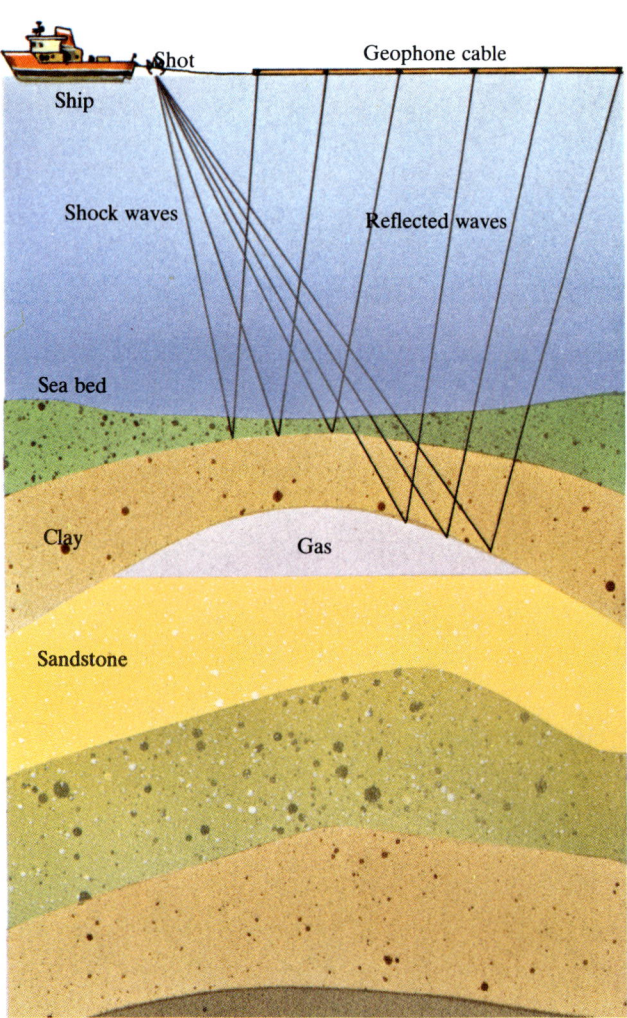

The sound waves from a seismic survey are monitored to assess the rock layers.

In such a survey, an explosion is set off on the ground or under the sea. A number of microphones (called geophones) measure the time it takes for the sound of the explosion to bounce off the layers of rock beneath the earth's crust. The signals from the geophones are fed into a computer which converts them into a picture of the rock layers.

Next an exploratory well is drilled to see if any oil or gas is actually there. A drilling rig or drillship will bore a hole through the rocks to

Above *Deeper waters are explored by a drill ship. The ship is kept in position with its propellors.*

depths of 3,000 metres (10,000 feet) or even 6,000 metres (20,000 feet). It is more common to find gas and oil together but gas can be discovered on its own, in what is called a 'gas field'.

On dry land a drilling rig can be set up on a convenient open space away from towns and houses. But when wells have to be drilled at sea, large floating drilling rigs are used, which have to be securely anchored to the sea-bed.

Left *Drilling for gas on land needs less preparation than an offshore project.*

3. Discovery and appraisal

Once gas has been discovered, it has to be brought to the surface. Before a decision can be taken to produce the gas, the company must calculate if the reserves are extensive enough to make the venture profitable. This means finding out if the value of the gas is greater than the cost of producing it.

A series of 'appraisal' wells are drilled around the area where the gas was discovered. This will show how large the reservoir is. Large fields can stretch for several kilometres. The next stage is to measure the rate at which gas flows out of the appraisal wells. The engineers can then work out how much gas is in the field. If the tests are favourable, production drilling begins.

A permanent structure has to be installed to control the flow of gas. If the well is on dry land this structure is called a 'Christmas tree'. It is

Offshore drilling for North Sea gas.

A production platform on Australia's North-West shelf.

simply a small assembly of valves and gauges.

On the other hand, the gasfield might be hundreds of kilometres from land, under water several hundred metres deep. In this case a very large platform will have to be securely fixed to the sea-bed.

The platform has living accommodation and a helicopter landing deck. It is also designed to withstand buffeting from waves 30 metres (100 feet) high.

In the future, gas is likely to be found in increasingly deep waters. To overcome this, the production platforms may be designed to float, attached to the sea bed only by strong wires.

A typical gas production platform. **Inset** *A rig compared to the Post Office Tower.*

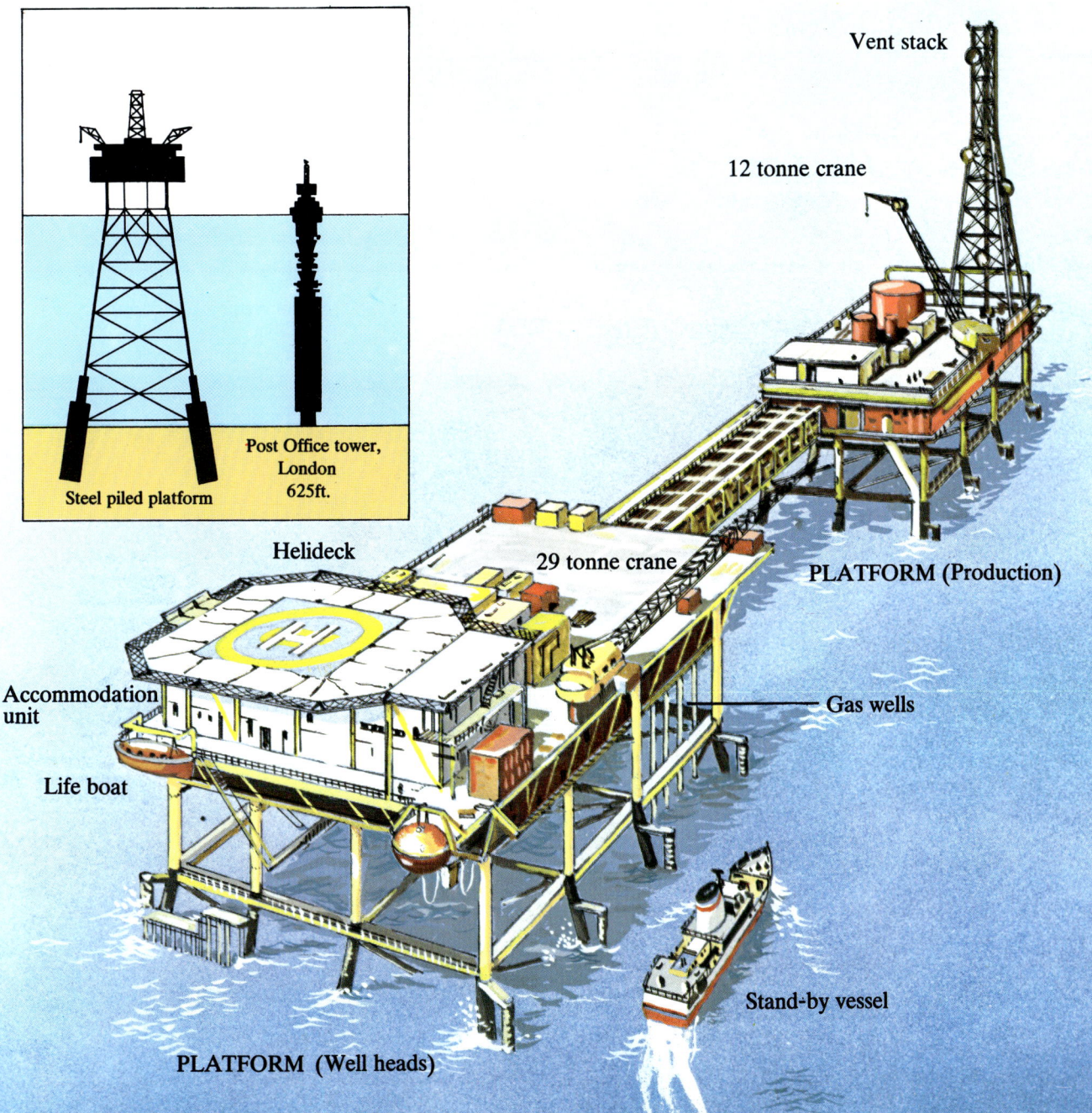

4. Transmission

Gas is rarely discovered in the places where people want to use it. Frequently it has to be transported over distances of hundreds of thousands of kilometres.

The simplest solution is to lay a high-pressure pipeline. This can send the gas over long distances for relatively low costs. It would be very expensive and inconvenient to send the same amount of gas by road or rail, for example.

However, once pipelines have been laid, it is

A transmission pipeline is laid with the help of crawler tractors.

impossible to send the gas to a different destination. For this reason pipelines are only laid when people are planning to send large quantities of gas for a period of 20 years or more.

Transmission pipelines can be laid in trenches on land and also on the sea-bed. On land the sections of steel pipe are welded together in long continuous lengths. A team of crawler tractors with large side arms lift the pipeline from the ground into the trench. Although steel is a very tough metal, it is flexible enough to bend around the curves of the trench.

An offshore pipeline is laid from a big floating vessel, called a laybarge. The pipeline is gradually lowered down to the sea-bed over a long boom, called a stinger, which prevents it bending too sharply as it leaves the laybarge.

Gas in an underground reservoir is under tremendous pressure which is sufficient to push it through the pipeline for long distances, but if the pipeline is very long it may be necessary to give the gas an additional 'push' with very powerful compressors.

Laying an offshore pipeline into the sea.

Below *From a laybarge the gas pipeline is gradually lowered onto the sea bed.*

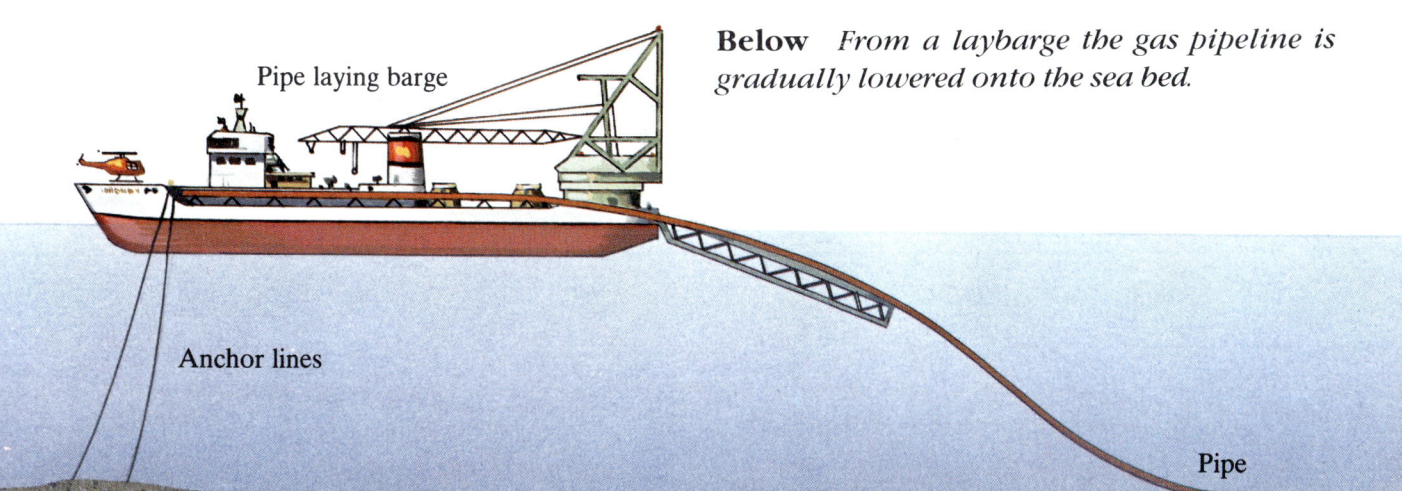

5. Distribution

Buried beneath our streets, pavements and gardens is a maze of gas mains, forming 'grids'. These grids transport gas from the supplier to the customer. Today gas mains are nearly always made from plastic, which is both tough and flexible. These are most important characteristics when transporting a gas, which could explode, in a highly populated area. Vibration from heavy lorries can cause considerable damage to such pipes.

It is important for gas mains to have very long working lives, with the minimum of maintenance. They are buried underground and it is inconvenient to dig them up for repair work.

Another advantage of the plastic gas mains is that the sections of pipe can be easily joined by melting (fusing) the ends together. Techniques of laying gas mains are continually being improved to reduce disruption in busy streets.

In some cases, new plastic gas mains can be inserted into old cast-iron gas mains without switching off the gas flow. This cuts out the need to dig up a whole road. Digging trenches in congested areas can also be avoided by using a 'mole'. This torpedo-shaped instrument bores a hole in the earth, and the gas main is simply inserted in its place.

Many major cities still have some gas mains which were laid 50 or 100 years ago. These were made from cast iron, a brittle material which easily cracks. The escaping gas from such a break can cause serious accidents. To avoid this danger the old gas mains have to be replaced with tough plastic ones.

Gas mains need to be hard-wearing, as maintenance disrupts busy streets.

A map showing the location of North Sea gas, along with its distribution.

6. The history of town gas

Long before natural gas was widely accepted as a clean and efficient fuel, there was a large industry producing gas from coal. The streets of London, in 1812, were the first in the world to be illuminated by town gas.

For many years before this, it was known that coal would give off a gas when it was heated. In 1792 a Scottish engineer, William Murdock, working in Redruth, Cornwall, used coal gas to light his house. Later, in 1804, an iron foundry in Birmingham installed a gas lighting system under Murdock's guidance.

This process, called carbonization, did not actually involve burning the coal. It was just heated, which broke down the chemicals into a range of different products.

In addition to gas, the process produced coke and a tarry liquid. The coke consisted of almost pure carbon and could be used as a fuel. The tar

An early cartoon commenting on the first gas street lights in London.

contained a number of chemicals which could be extracted to make dyes and explosives.

The early gas 'undertakings', as the companies were called, were very local in nature. It was easier to transport coal to each town and city to make the gas on the spot than it would have been to send the gas long distances through pipelines.

In the early days of the town gas industry, the biggest use was for lighting streets and homes. Later on during the twentieth century electricity became more effective for lighting.

As the use of gas for lighting declined, its popularity as a fuel for cooking, heating rooms and hot water increased.

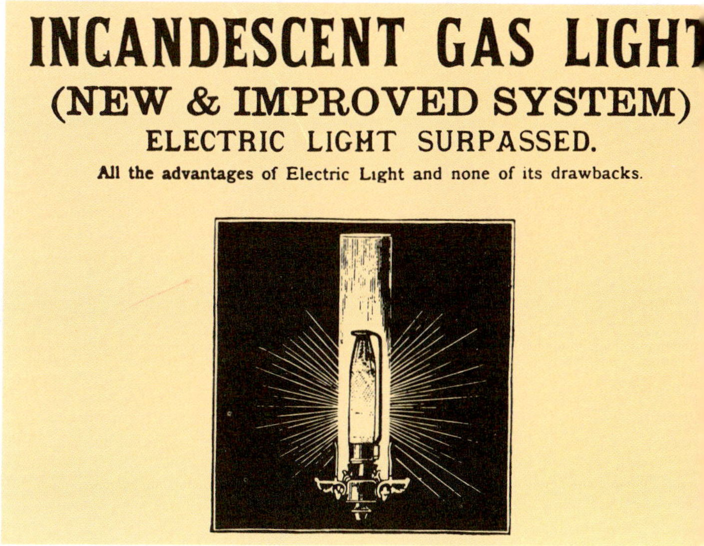

Below *A decorated gasometer of the 1930s; town gas was still used as street lighting.*

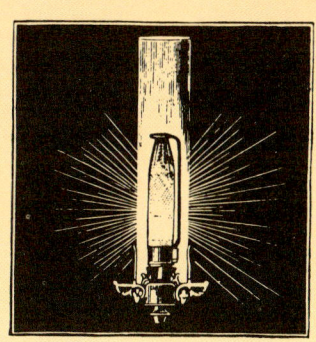

Above *Electricity became a serious competitor to gas lighting.*

7. Gas in the home

Many people appreciate the benefits of using gas in their homes today. The biggest growth has taken place since the price of oil from the Middle East increased sharply during the 1970s. Gas quickly gained an advantage when compared with the price of other household fuels.

Gas is still very popular for cooking.

A gas cooker of the 1920s.

Ever since the earliest days of the gas industry in the nineteenth century, gas has been used for cooking. Probably its biggest attraction is the ability to control the amount of heat quickly by simply turning a knob.

Gas is also widely used for heating water in kitchens and bathrooms. Modern designs of heaters can produce large quantities of steaming water in an instant.

Another attractive use of gas in the home is for heating rooms. The wall heater is very compact and is much more efficient than an open coal fire which sends a lot of heat straight up the chimney. But, perhaps the most widespread use of gas in the home is for central heating. This is an extremely convenient way of heating every room in the house from one central boiler.

The boiler heats water, which is piped to a radiator in each room. The radiators have a large surface area so the heat from the water quickly passes into the air of the room. The water is then pumped from the radiator to the boiler, to be heated up once again. The central-heating boiler can also provide hot water for the household by heating water in a separate tank.

Central heating radiators help to keep every room at a constant temperature.

8. Gas in industry and commerce

Gas is an ideal fuel for many uses in industry and commerce. The reasons why gas is used for so many different processes is because it is so easy to control. It is possible to design burners of different sizes and shapes which give just the right amount of heat in the right places. When light bulbs are made, gas is used to heat the glass to exactly the right temperature for moulding.

On a larger scale, burners are incorporated into furnaces, ovens, kilns and boilers. Many factories need lots of hot water and steam. Some factories need hot air for drying paint on new cars; others need hot ovens to cook millions of biscuits, cakes and bread.

A great deal of gas is used for heating in large offices, hospitals and public buildings, like

This factory boiler room uses gas to heat its offices and workshops.

theatres. It is also very popular for cooking in hotels and restaurants where meals have to be prepared for many people.

The heart of any oven, furnace or boiler is the burner. This has to be carefully designed to mix air and gas together in just the right quantities to make sure all the energy is used. All burners must be able to work equally well when they are producing a lot of heat or a little.

This ability is described as the turn-down

Below *In the production of aerosols a special type of gas is used.*

Above *Accurately positioned gas jets help to mould these spotlights.*

ratio. A cooker, with a turn-down ratio of 10 means each burner gives 10 times as much heat with the biggest flame, as compared to the smallest one.

In the industrial production of aerosols a special type of gas is used, which is forced under pressure into the can. When the release nozzle is pushed the gas escapes along with the aerosol contents.

9. Metering

Everyone wants to know how much gas they are buying or selling. A liquid can be put in a measuring jug, a solid can be weighed, but measuring gas is more difficult. A gas will change its volume with even the smallest variation in pressure or temperature.

Further complications arise from the very wide range of conditions in which gas is measured. On the one hand, people need to know how much gas a central heating boiler is using. Yet at the other extreme, gas from an underground reservoir at very high pressure and flow rates also has to be measured accurately. It is impossible to find one meter which will satisfy all needs.

A high pressure pipeline uses a system of 'orifice plates'. A plate with a hole in the middle is placed in the pipe. These plates can be changed; a plate with a smaller hole will slow down the gas flow, while a larger hole will allow the gas to flow faster. Careful measurement of the flow rate can then be calculated.

Sophisticated computers chart the flow of gas from offshore transmission pipelines.

A 'turbine meter' depends on a propeller which rotates. As the gas passes through, it causes the blades of the turbine to turn. The speed of rotation tells how much gas is flowing.

Yet another way of metering is called 'vortex shedding'. It is an ingenious method as it has no moving parts. A small barrier creates turbulence and causes the gas stream to move from side to side. The speed of this 'to and fro'

Below *A cross-section through a pipeline which uses orifice plates. A plate with a large hole is being inserted, enabling the gas to flow faster.*

Above *A type of coin-operated gas meter found in the home.*

movement is used to calculate how fast the gas is flowing.

The meter in our homes uses a rubber diaphragm like a bellows. The gas expands the diaphragm and operates levers which drive a counter. It is a simple idea, and is very reliable.

10. Safety and gas detection

This explosion in 1985 was due to a cracked cast-iron gas main.

Fuel gases are valuable because they burn rapidly and give out plenty of heat. This can also be their biggest drawback. If the combustion gets out of control it can lead to an explosion.

One of the best ways of ensuring maximum safety is to detect the slightest leak of gas before the situation gets out of hand. If a gas leak is suspected, a specialized team is called to search for the tiniest trace of gas that may have come from a broken gas main. Workmen installing gas equipment in houses and factories also carry hand detectors to pick up signs of leakage.

Gas-detection equipment is installed permanently in such places as offshore platforms where there is a higher chance of finding gas. These detectors are switched on day and night and will sound an alarm if the amount of gas rises above a certain level.

Some fuel gases are lighter than air, so a gas detector is fitted at the highest point in the room. When the gas is heavier than air, the detector must be placed at the lowest point.

A gas detector works on a relatively simple principle. In the middle of the detector is a 'pellistor', consisting of a platinum wire filament coated with a special chemical. This wire is very delicate, being finer than a human hair.

When a fuel gas touches the pellistor it changes the electrical current passing through the wire. This change is either shown on a dial or will trigger an alarm. More sophisticated detectors will also operate safety devices.

Detecting a gas leak at the earliest possible moment is vital. This diagram illustrates how some gas detectors work.

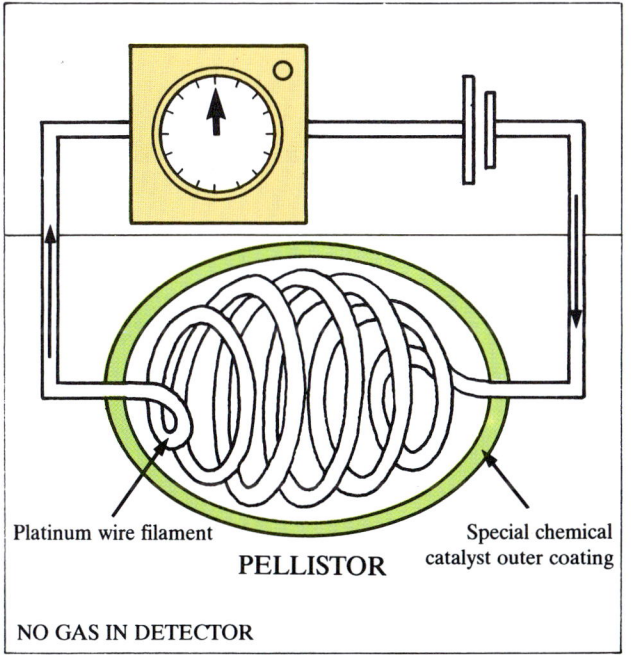
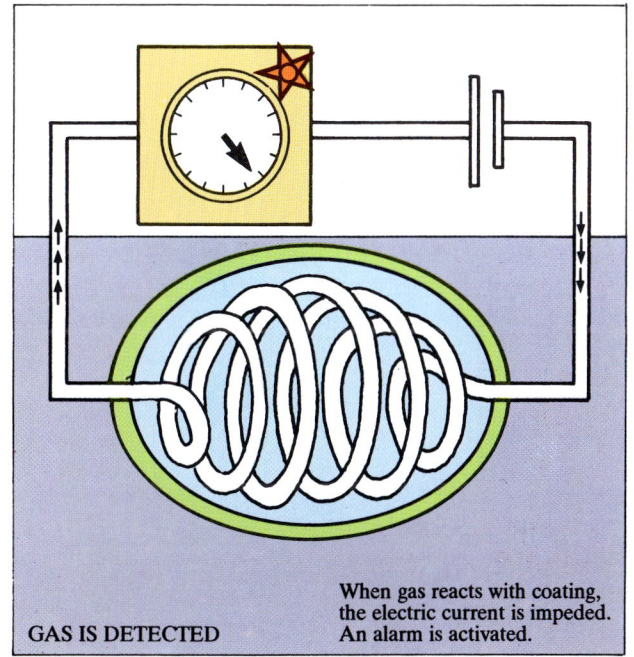

11. How gas is stored

There is a wide variation in the amount of gas used during the course of any day. Seasonal changes are also noticeable. The usage can be five times higher in winter than in summer.

These big differences can be smoothed out by storing enough gas so that it can be quickly called upon when required.

Storage can take a number of forms. Many people will have seen the large gasometers in their town, which have roofs that rise and fall as they fill up and empty.

Gas can also be stored in liquefied natural gas (LNG) tanks. The LNG tanks also hold much larger quantities than the gasometer because the gas is in liquid form.

It is not always possible to see where gas is being stored. Sometimes it is stored in a gasfield which has been specially adapted. In this case

Gasometers are a common way of storing gas in towns.

A cavern in Lavera, France, during excavation. It will soon be used for storing gas.

gas is pumped into the permeable sponge-like rocks under the ground and pumped out again when it is needed.

In other cases large cavities, as big as a cathedral, can be formed underground and the gas pumped in. This can be done in rock layers made of salt. Sea water is pumped underground to dissolve the salt which then leaves a big hole, forming a useful storage space.

Another form of storage which cannot be seen is called 'line-pack' storage. The pressure of gas inside a pipeline can be increased above the normal level. A lot more gas can be 'packed' into the pipeline in this way.

This terminal in Dorset, England, stores gas from a nearby inland production well.

12. Liquefied natural gas (LNG)

All gases can be converted into liquids if they are 'squeezed' under sufficiently high pressure. In practice though, a very high pressure would be required to turn methane gas into a liquid.

It is easier to cool methane down to below its boiling point ($-160°C$, $-256°F$) so that the gas condenses into a liquid. Once the natural gas is at this temperature, it does not need additional pressure to keep it liquid.

It is most important to prevent the very cold LNG warming up, otherwise the liquid will start to boil and could be lost. For this reason LNG tanks have to be insulated thoroughly with thick cladding.

The big advantage of converting methane into a liquid is that it occupies much less space. The volume of the liquid is only one-six hundredth of the same quantity of gas.

This property is most useful for storing large

Under high pressure, gases convert to liquids.

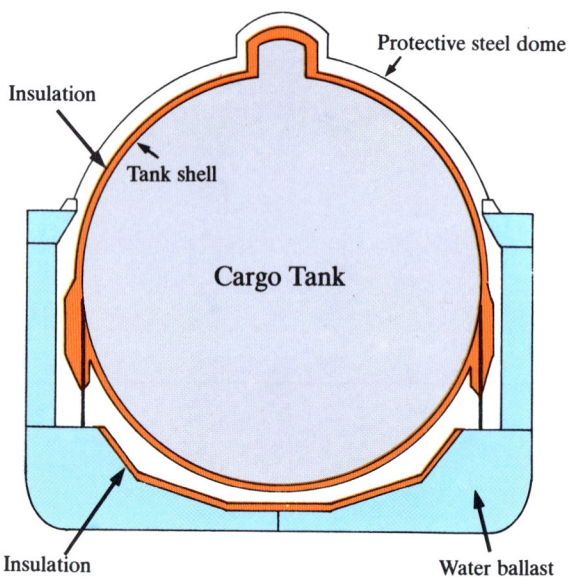

A cross-section of an LNG tanker.

quantities of gas and also transporting it over long distances. Natural gas can be conveniently stored in LNG tanks during the summer months when less gas is used. Then during the cold winter months the LNG can be turned back into gas by warming it up when people need it to heat their homes.

LNG is also the only satisfactory way of sending sizeable quantities of gas long distances across the oceans of the world. It simply would not be feasible to lay pipelines. Big ships containing large tanks are used to carry LNG hundreds and even thousands of kilometres.

A refrigerated LNG carrier is the only practical way of transporting vast quantities of gas across the oceans of the world.

13. Liquefied petroleum gas (LPG)

Above *Large amounts of LPG are stored in these spherical tanks.*

Propane and butane are two hydrocarbon gases which will turn to liquid under relatively moderate pressure. This useful feature means that the gases can be transported in cylinders and tanks.

A lot of liquefied petroleum gas (LPG) is transported around the world in ships which have large tanks. LPGs can also be transported on land in road tankers and in small cylinders which are convenient to use in houses and factories.

The LPGs are obtained as by-products from the refining of crude oil. They are also obtained from oil and gas wells. They can be used as a fuel in almost exactly the same way as natural gas. People in remote country areas use LPG to heat their homes when they cannot be reached by gas mains.

Below *LPG carriers are different from LNG ships as refrigeration is not necessary.*

In a number of countries, LPG is used as a fuel to power cars and vans because it is sometimes cheaper than petrol. Another advantage is that it burns cleanly and, therefore, lengthens the life of the engine.

Industry uses LPG whenever fuel is needed for a short period, such as on a building site. It might be used for cooking meals for construction workers or melting bitumen.

This farmer uses a LPG heater to provide warmth for his recently hatched pheasants.

LPG tankers supply country areas which are not connected to the gas mains.

Farmers use a lot of LPG for drying grain, heating animal pens and for heating greenhouses.

There are also many other uses for small quantities of LPG fuel. It provides energy for a wide range of items: from camping stoves to do-it-yourself blowlamps, and more recently butane-filled hair tongs.

14. Compressed natural gas (CNG)

Compressed natural gas (CNG) is growing in importance in some parts of the world as a fuel for cars, lorries and buses. It is popular in the USA, Canada, Italy, New Zealand and the USSR. The vehicles carry very tough cyclinders into which natural gas is pumped at very high pressures, up to 200 times more than atmospheric pressure.

One of the benefits of using CNG as a vehicle fuel is that the exhaust gases do not cause as much pollution as petrol (gasoline). Drivers of CNG vehicles can refill their cylinders at special filling stations by the side of the road. Alternatively they can fill up at night from the gas supply to their homes. All they need is a small compressor to pump the gas into the cylinder at

A car, converted to CNG, is refilled at a special service station in Canada.

the high pressure required.

CNG is used in some countries which have a plentiful supply of natural gas. Other countries use CNG as a car fuel because it saves money, for without CNG they would have to use expensive imported petrol.

Although there are savings on fuel bills, there are some drawbacks. It is not possible to drive the vehicle outside the area covered by CNG service stations. To overcome this some vehicles are converted to use either CNG or petrol.

Another problem is reduced power. For this reason CNG is mainly used by companies who operate fleets of delivery vans or lorries which do not need fast acceleration.

A traditional petrol engine which has been modified to run on gas.

15. Substitute natural gas (SNG)

As this London gasworks shows, the carbonization of coal used to be the only way of producing gas.

Substitute natural gas is a fuel gas which can be made from either oil or coal. It can be mixed with natural gas to boost supplies when demand is high in the cold winter months.

Substitute natural gas usually costs more than natural gas because the oil 'base' is very expensive. For this reasons SNG is normally used only as a substitute in times of shortage.

Compared to the amount of natural gas that is used around the world, the amount of SNG used is very small. However, it may become more important in the future.

At the moment there are plentiful supplies of natural gas in many countries. But one day all this will be burnt. It may then be possible to manufacture substitute natural gas from coal because there is enough coal in the world to last for a very long time.

This could then be a very efficient way of sending the energy of coal to people who want to use it. SNG would be made in very large plants like oil refineries.

Another possibility would be to convert the coal to gas without digging it up. This is being tried in some countries to see if it can be made to work. The coal has to be heated up deep underground so that it is converted into gas. The gas is then brought to the surface through a borehole. There are a number of problems in this method, so it may be several years before it is successful.

Right *The stages of SNG production.*

Below *Britain's Westfield centre is developing ways of producing SNG efficiently.*

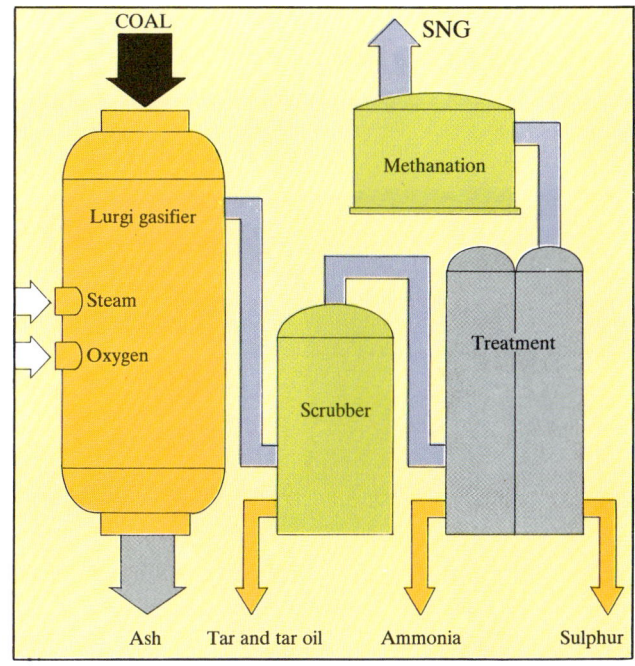

16. Biogas

Above *A modern digester is often used on farms, processing animal waste to provide methane, which in turn produces electricity from a generator (on the right in this picture).*

Methane gas is produced when waste material from animals and plants is broken down by certain bacteria. These bacteria work fast in anaerobic conditions, that is in the absence of oxygen.

This process is utilised to deal with sewage from towns. The process of anaerobic decomposition is also used to generate methane gas deliberately from animal manure. This method has become particularly popular on farms which have many pigs, cattle or poultry.

The manure is put into a large tank, called a 'digester'. Here, the bacteria multiply and break down the animal waste, if the contents of the digester are kept warm.

The methane from the digester is fed to an

Above *A methane digester in India.*

These landfill sites contain thousands of tonnes of waste and can be several hundred metres deep. When the pit is full, a layer of clay is spread over the top to keep the air out. Very soon the bacteria begin to produce methane. Large quantities of gas can be piped to factories for many years and help to save fuel costs.

Below *A landfill site. After covering waste with clay, anaerobic decomposition begins. Here, a trial flare is testing for methane.*

engine which generates electricity. Sufficient electricity is generated to power the equipment and pumps of the digester plant with some electricity left over. The waste heat from the generator is piped back to the digester to keep it warm.

The solid material remaining after digestion is complete contains some organic matter, but has little smell. It can be spread on farmland as fertilizer.

Anaerobic decomposition is also important in producing methane at 'landfill' sites, where refuse from our homes, containing a high proportion of organic material, is tipped into deep pits or quarries.

17. The manufacture of chemicals

The Fife ethylene plant in Scotland is being developed to utilize gas resources from the nearby Brent field (see map on page 15).

The fuel gases can be used to make chemicals as well as to produce energy. As we explained in chapter 1, hydrocarbons, like crude oil and the fuel gases, are made from two elements — hydrogen and carbon. These chemicals can be rearranged in almost limitless ways, each combination making a different chemical.

A lot of common materials are produced from hydrocarbon sources. Plastic is a material found in numerous different forms in everyday life, from packaging to car interiors. Paints and synthetic fabrics are just two other examples of the 'petrochemical' industry.

These products are made in large chemical plants. By using very high temperatures and pressures, the molecules of the hydrocarbons can be broken up and put back together in different ways.

Methane can be used to produce a range of useful industrial solvents by reacting it with chlorine gas. Methane is also the starting material to produce methyl alcohol which is useful as a chemical 'intermediate' in the manufacture of other chemicals. Methane, too, is used to produce ammonia which is a vital ingredient of the fertilizers which farmers use.

Another hydrocarbon gas, ethane, is used as the starting point for a number of widely used products. Ethane contains two carbon atoms and six hydrogen atoms. If the ethane is passed through a hot furnace, called a 'cracker', the

After passing through a 'cracker', ethylene is treated in a fractionating tower — like the one under construction in the picture.

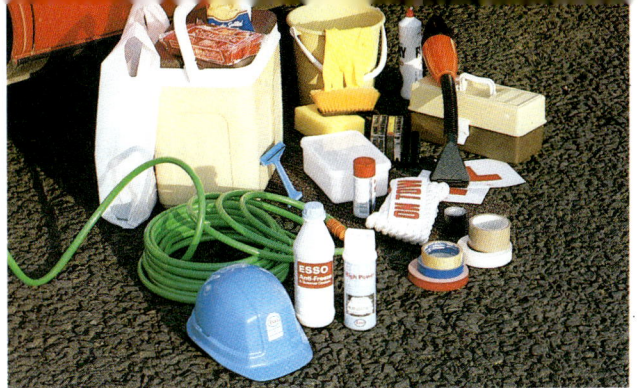

Examples of products made from ethylene.

molecule can be 'cracked' and two hydrogen atoms removed.

The molecule produced from the cracker is ethylene. It is used to produce PVC plastic, polyethylene plastic, polystyrene plastic, and ethylene glycol which is used as antifreeze in car radiators.

18. International trade

A lot of gas is bought and sold between different countries. In spite of this, gas is not an easy commodity to trade internationally.

The two main methods of transporting gases over long distances take a great deal of preparation and money, so to make it worthwhile agreements have to last for as long as 20 years. Once transmission pipelines are laid, they are virtually fixed.

The LNG ships can only travel between a certain number of points. At the point of departure, the gas has to be cooled down in a large 'liquefaction' plant and an equally large 'gasification' plant is needed on arrival to convert the liquid back to gas.

A gas pipeline being laid in the USSR.

International trade agreements have to be longterm, as gas pipelines, like these in New Zealand, are very expensive to lay.

Despite these difficulties, more and more gas is being traded. The USSR has the largest gas reserves in the world. It sells gas through pipelines to several countries in Western Europe, such as France, West Germany and Italy.

Norway has much gas in its sector of the North Sea and sells this to its neighbours.

A pipeline under the Mediterranean, has

been laid so that Italy can buy gas from Algeria.

Japan already buys a lot of LNG from Indonesia, Abu Dhabi and Brunei because it has little gas of its own. It plans to buy even more from Australia and Canada. The USA buys gas from Canada and Mexico through pipelines.

Nigeria has plenty of gas which is not being used. Plans have been discussed to build a pipeline one day across the Sahara Desert to send the gas to customers in Europe.

The Senboku gas works near Osaka in Japan, stores imported gas from a number of countries.

19. Gas industries around the world

Gas is used in many countries of the world. The biggest gas industry in the world is in the USA. The country has large gas reserves but still has to buy gas from its neighbours. There are hundreds of gas utilities (companies) which distribute gas to a particular town, city or county.

In Britain and France there is just one utility for the whole country. These companies are owned by the government. They are large organizations, which deal with every aspect of the gas industry from exploration to selling gas cookers. The British Government has now put forward plans to sell the British Gas Corporation to anyone who wants to buy a share of it.

The USSR has the largest gas reserves with more than one-third of the world's total. But,

The British Gas Corporation sells gas appliances in shops such as these as well as supplying gas.

Above *A construction team in the USSR surveying a new gas pipeline in Siberia.*

Below *Gas being burnt by 'flaring'; some countries now utilize this by-product of oil.*

much of this gas is in the frozen Arctic Circle and has to be sent thousands of kilometres by pipelines. More than 90 per cent of homes in the USSR use gas because the government supplies it cheaply.

Many countries of the world are now planning new gas industries, for two main reasons. Firstly, because they find it is a cheaper fuel than oil and secondly to try and utilize the gas produced as a by-product of oil. This is often just wastefully burnt away in a process called 'flaring'. Saudi Arabia, for example, uses such gas to manufacture chemicals which are then profitably exported.

Facts and figures

Percentage share of the world's gas reserves

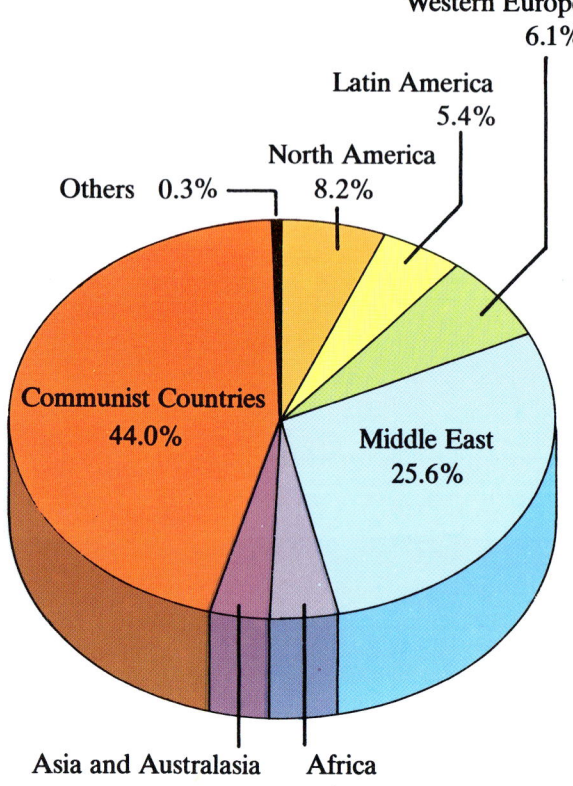

Reserves of Natural Gas (1984)

COUNTRY	TRILLION CUBIC FEET*	R/P RATIO
NORTH AMERICA		
USA	198.0	
Canada	92.3	
Total	290.3	14.7
LATIN AMERICA		
Mexico	77.0	
Venezuela	55.4	
Others	52.5	
Total	184.9	66.4
WESTERN EUROPE		
Norway	89.0	
Netherlands	68.5	
United Kingdom	25.6	
Others	23.5	
Total	206.6	34.3
MIDDLE EAST		
Iran	478.6	
Qatar	150.0	
Saudi Arabia	123.3	
Others	117.5	
Total	869.4	100+
AFRICA		
Algeria	109.1	
Nigeria	35.6	
Libya	21.2	
Others	21.3	
Total	187.2	100+
ASIA & AUSTRALASIA		
Malaysia	50.0	
Indonesia	40.0	
Australia	17.8	
Others	58.4	
Total	166.2	62.3
COMMUNIST COUNTRIES		
USSR	1,450.0	
China	30.9	
Others	14.3	
Total	1,495.2	65.5
TOTAL WORLD	**3,399.8**	**60.0**

The R/P ratio, shown on the chart, indicates how long, in years, remaining gas reserves will last if production continues at the current rate.

* Trillion being equal to a million × million.

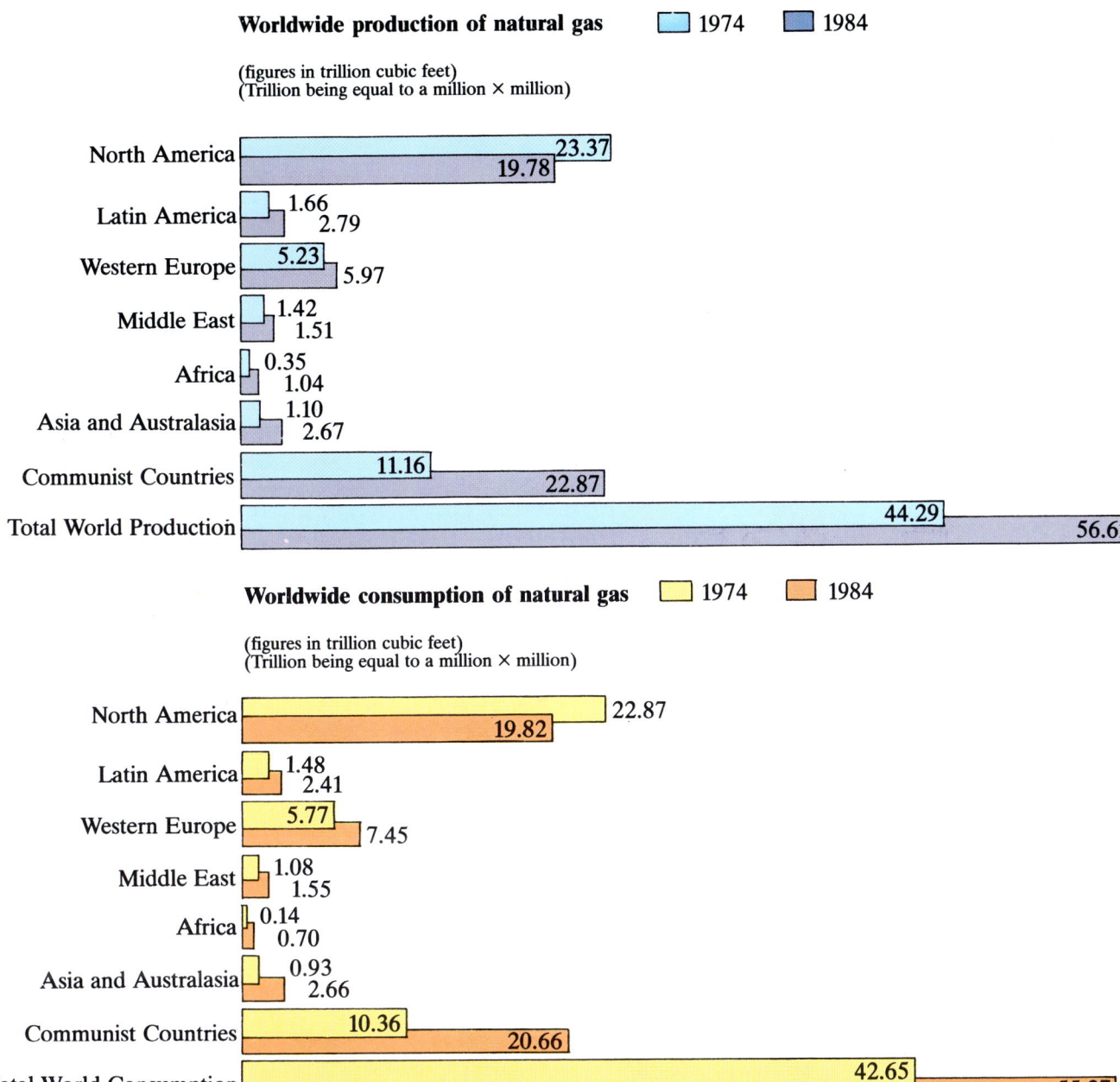

Source: *BP Statistical Review of World Energy*, June 1985

Glossary

Appraisal well A well drilled to estimate the quantity of oil or gas in a reservoir.

Atmospheric pressure The air pressure at sea level.

Butane A hydrocarbon gas which is easily converted to liquid under pressure. One of the gases known as liquefied petroleum gas (LPG).

'Christmas tree structure' A system of pipes and valves fitted to production wells to control the flow of oil or gas.

Compressor Equipment to 'squeeze' gas to drive it through a pipeline.

Condensate Gases produced from an oil or gas well which readily condense into liquids on emerging from the well.

'Cracker' A furnace which breaks hydrocarbon molecules into smaller ones.

Crude oil Oil in its natural state, as it is found in the ground. It mainly consists of hydrocarbons which have to be refined to be of any use.

Ethane A hydrocarbon gas which is more frequently used to produce chemicals than as a fuel.

Exploratory well A well drilled to search for new reservoirs of oil or gas.

'Flaring' The burning of surplus gas at an oil production well.

Gasification The manufacture of a gaseous fuel from a solid or liquid fuel.

Gas main A pipe used to transport gas at low pressure.

Geophone A microphone used in seismic surveys to pick up the sound waves reflected from rock layers beneath the earth's surface.

Hydrocarbons The compounds consisting only of the elements hydrogen and carbon, which can exist in the form of solids, liquids or gases.

'Line-pack' The storage of gas in a pipeline by raising the pressure above its normal operating pressure.

Liquefied natural gas (LNG) Natural gas that has been liquefied by refrigeration. Natural gas condenses into a liquid at −160°C.

Liquefied petroleum gas (LPG) The hydrocarbon gases (propane and butane) which become liquid under the effect of moderate pressure.

Methane A hydrocarbon gas. It forms the major part of natural gas

Molecule A group of two or more atoms, held together by chemical bonds.

Natural gas A naturally occurring range of gases consisting mainly of methane but with small, quantities of other hydrocarbon gases such as ethane, propane, and butane. In the gas supply industry, the term 'natural gas' is assumed to refer to a mixture consisting mainly of methane.

Pipeline A pipe through which gas or liquid is transported from one place to another.

Platform A permanent offshore structure from which wells can be drilled and oil or gas can be produced.

Production drilling Drilling of wells to bring a field into production.

Propane A hydrocarbon gas which can be converted to liquid under pressure and is one of the constituents of liquefied petroleum gas (LPG).

Reservoir A layer of rock in which oil or gas is present.

Seismic survey A system of determining the structure of rock layers by measuring reflected shock waves.

Substitute natural gas (SNG) The gas produced from coal or oil which has similar characteristics as natural gas.

Town gas The fuel gas manufactured by carbonizing coal. It contained a mixture of gases including hydrogen, methane and carbon monoxide. Now it is largely superceded by natural gas as a fuel.

Transmission The bulk movement of gas through high pressure pipelines.

Sources of further information

Your regional gas board may be able to provide you with information of a local nature, while the British Gas Corporation have an educational department which can supply booklets and leaflets on various aspects of the gas industry on request.

Some useful addresses:

North Thames Gas, North Thames House,
London Road, Staines,
Middlesex TW18 4AE

British Gas Educational Service,
PO Box 46, Hounslow, Middlesex TW4 6NF

Several of the large oil companies also provide educational material on gas;

BP Educational Service, Britannic House,
Moor Lane, London EC2

Books to read

ADAMS, H. *Gas and its Uses* (Blackwell-Raintree)
ARNOLD, G. *Gas* (Franklin Watts)
CASSIDY, R. *Gas Natural Energy* (Frederick Muller)
HARDY, D. *Energy and the Future* (World's Work)
LARSON, E. *New Sources of Energy and Power* (Frederick Muller)
LUCAS, A. & D. *The Gas in your Home* (Wayland)
MITCHELL, V. *Picture Book of Authentic Mid-Victorian Gas Lighting Fixtures* (Dover Publications)
PEEBLES, M. *Evolution of the Gas Industry* (Macmillan)
PENNER, S. *New Sources of Oil and Gas* (Pergamon Press)
THOMAS, J. *The Quest for Fuel* (Wayland)
WILLIAMS, T. *A History of the British Gas Industry* (Oxford University Press)

Picture acknowledgements

The author and publishers would like to thank the following for allowing their illustrations to be reproduced in this book: AMEC plc 12; Bibby Bros. & Co. 30 (right); Biomass International 36 (left); British Gas Corporation 17 (top), 19, 35; British Petroleum *frontispiece*, 8, 10 (both), 21 (left), 26 (top), 27, 29, 43 (bottom); Calor Gas 31 (both); Canadian Gas Association 32; Essochem Olefins Inc. 38, 39 (both); Captain R.G. Hodgkinson 9 (right); Land Fill Gas Ltd 37; The Mansell Collection 17 (bottom), 34; North Thames Gas 14, 18 (right), 20, 26 (bottom), 42; Novosti Press Agency 40 (bottom); Osaka Gas Company Ltd. 41; PHOTRI 28; Picturepoint 9 (left); The Press Association 24; Shell photographs 7, 13, 22, 30 (left), 33; Thorn EMI Domestic Appliances Ltd. 18 (left); Thorn EMI Flow Measurements Ltd. 23 (right); Thorn EMI Lighting Ltd. 21 (right); Wayland Picture Library 16, 37 (top), 40 (top). The illustrations on pages 6, 7, 8, 11, 13, 15, 23, 25, 28 and 35 are by Malcolm S. Walker.

Index

Aerosols 21
Algeria 40, 44
Anaerobic decomposition 36, 37
Australia 10, 41, 44

Biogas 36
Boilers 19, 20
Britain 42, 44
Burners 21

Canada 32, 41, 44
Cap rock 8, 46
Carbonization 16
Central heating 19, 22
Chemical manufacture 38–39, 43
   'cracker' furnace 39, 46
   'fractionating' tower 39
Coal gas 16, 34
Compressed natural gas (CNG) 32–33
Cooking, gas 17, 18, 21, 31
Crude oils 6, 7, 30, 39, 46

Drilling 7, 8, 9, 10, 46
Drillships 9

Electricity 17, 36
Explosions 14, 24

Fife ethylene plant 38–39
'Flaring' gas 43, 46
France 40, 42

Gas
   discovery 10, 12
   distribution 14–15
   exploration 6, 8, 42
   in the future 10, 34
   in the home 17, 18, 19, 31
   lighting 16–17
   terminals 27

   trading 40–41
   transportation 12–13, 14, 40
Gas, types of
   butane 7, 30, 46
   ethane 7, 39, 46
   methane 6, 28, 36, 37
   propane 7, 30, 46
Gas cap 8
Gas flow 10, 14, 23
Gas leak detection 24–25
Gas mains 14, 46
Gas utilities 42
Gasfields 9, 10
Gasification and liquefication plants 38, 46
Geophones 9, 46

Hydrocarbons 6, 39, 46

Industry 20–21

Japan 39

Landfill sites 37
Liquefied natural gas (LNG) 28–29, 46
Liquefied petroleum gas (LPG) 30–31, 46
LNG ships 28–29, 40
LPG ships 30

Metering
   in the home 23
   'orifice plates' 22
   'turbine meters' 23
   'vortex shedding' 23
Mexico 41, 44
Middle East 18, 44–45
Murdock, William 16

Natural gas 8, 16, 30, 33, 34, 46
   consumption 45
   production 45

reserves 15, 44
New Zealand 32, 40
Nigeria 39, 44
Norway 40, 44

Oil 8, 9, 34
Oil companies 8

Pipelines 40, 46
   high-pressure 12–13, 22
   offshore 13
   under Mediterranean 40
Production platform 10–11, 25

Rock layers 8–9

Saudi Arabia 43, 44
Scotland 38–39
Seismic survey 8–9, 46
Storage
   caverns 26–27
   gasometers 17, 26
   'Line-pack' 26, 46
   LNG tanks 27
   LPG tanks 30
Substitute natural gas (SNG) 34–35, 46

Town gas 16–17, 46
Transmission 12, 13, 46
'Turn-down ratio' 21

USA 32, 40, 42, 44
USSR 32, 40, 42, 44

Vehicle fuels 31, 32–33

Wells 30
   'appraisal' 10, 46
   exploration 6, 9, 46
West Germany 40